What Does It Mean to Go Green?

Molly Aloian

Crabtree Publishing Company

www.crabtreebooks.com

Author
Molly Aloian

Publishing plan research and development
Reagan Miller

Editors
Rachel Eagen, Crystal Sikkens

Proofreader and indexer
Wendy Scavuzzo

Design
Samara Parent

Photo research
Crystal Sikkens

Production coordinator and prepress technician
Samara Parent

Print coordinator
Margaret Amy Salter

Photographs
istockphoto: cover (kids)
Thinkstock: title page, pages 3, 5 (right), 6, 14, 15, 16 (middle and
    right), 17, 18 (top left, bottom right), 19 (top), 20, 21, 22
Shutterstock: ©Shamleen/Shutterstock.com: page 9
All other images by Shutterstock

Library and Archives Canada Cataloguing in Publication

Aloian, Molly, author
    What does it mean to go green? / Molly Aloian.

(The green scene)
Includes index.
Issued in print and electronic formats.
ISBN 978-0-7787-0275-7 (bound).--ISBN 978-0-7787-0286-3
(pbk.).-- ISBN 978-1-4271-1271-2 (pdf).--ISBN 978-1-4271-0558-5
(html)

    1. Sustainable living--Juvenile literature. I. Title.

GE195.5.A563 2013   j333.72   C2013-905217-8
                                            C2013-905218-6

Library of Congress Cataloging-in-Publication Data

Aloian, Molly.
    What does it mean to go green? / Molly Aloian.
        pages cm. -- (The green scene)
    Includes index.
    ISBN 978-0-7787-0275-7 (reinforced library binding) -- ISBN 978-0-7787-
0286-3 (pbk.) -- ISBN 978-1-4271-1271-2 (electronic pdf) -- ISBN 978-1-4271-
0558-5 (electronic html)
    1. Environmentalism--Juvenile literature. 2. Sustainable living--Juvenile
literature. I. Title.

GE195.5.A48 2013
646.70028'6--dc23
                                            2013030089

Crabtree Publishing Company

www.crabtreebooks.com   1-800-387-7650

Printed in Canada/092013/BF20130815

Published in Canada
Crabtree Publishing
616 Welland Ave.
St. Catharines, Ontario
L2M 5V6

Published in the United States
Crabtree Publishing
PMB 59051
350 Fifth Avenue, 59th Floor
New York, New York 10118

Published in the United Kingdom
Crabtree Publishing
Maritime House
Basin Road North, Hove
BN41 1WR

Published in Australia
Crabtree Publishing
3 Charles Street
Coburg North
VIC 3058

Contents

DONATIONS

Earth in trouble

Every day, we do things that harm Earth. We waste energy and water, cause **pollution**, throw away too much garbage, and cut down trees. These are just a few of Earth's problems we are creating.

Too much garbage harms Earth's land, water, and living things.

Not the same

If we do not respect planet Earth and keep it healthy, plants, animals, and people will not have a safe place to live. Pollution will increase and garbage will pile up. We will run out of **natural resources**. Earth as we know it will not be the same.

Going green

Have you ever heard of "going green"? Going green means changing how you live, and how much you buy and throw away. It means using less energy and trying to **conserve**, or protect, all of Earth's natural resources. The Three Rs—**Reduce**, **Reuse**, and **Recycle**—are another part of going green.

*Going green lessens your **impact** on Earth. For example, use reusable containers for your school lunches to create less garbage!*

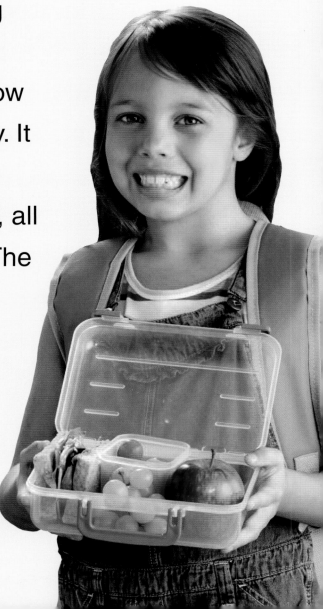

Take Action!

Trees are an important natural resource. Trees help clean the air and give us materials such as paper and wood. Can you think of ways to conserve this natural resource?

Fossil fuels are **non-renewable** natural resources that are burned to fuel cars, heat homes, and supply electricity. Appliances that are plugged into wall outlets, such as toasters and computers, use electricity. Burning fossil fuels creates air pollution.

Save electricity and reduce pollution by shutting off lights, TVs, and computers when you are not using them.

Earth hour

Near the end of March each year, people around the world participate in Earth Hour. During Earth Hour, people turn off their lights for one hour of the day. They do this to raise awareness about pollution and **global warming**.

9

Water worries

Water is a natural resource that we use every day. We use huge amounts of water without realizing how precious it is. Only one percent of all the water on Earth is available as fresh water for people to use. Saving water is a big part of going green.

Collect rain water in buckets to water your plants instead of using water from your tap.

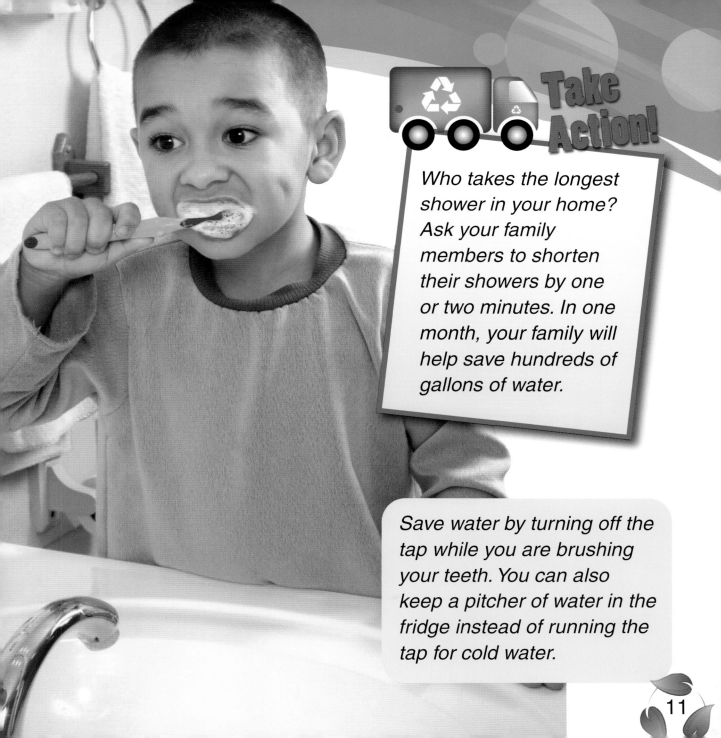

Take Action!

Who takes the longest shower in your home? Ask your family members to shorten their showers by one or two minutes. In one month, your family will help save hundreds of gallons of water.

Save water by turning off the tap while you are brushing your teeth. You can also keep a pitcher of water in the fridge instead of running the tap for cold water.

11

Keep it clean

Harmful **fumes**, waste, and chemicals from cars, ships, airplanes, and other vehicles cause pollution every day. This pollution creates global warming. Global warming heats up Earth and can make it hard for plants, animals, and even people to survive.

Riding your bicycle to school is a simple way to keep the air, land, and water clean.

Many people plant trees on Earth Day.

Earth Day

Earth Day is on April 22 each year. On that day, people all over the world remember to help Earth. Some Earth Day activities include picking up litter in your neighborhood, riding your bicycle to school, or shutting off your computer for the entire day.

Reducing

Reducing means using less. It is a big part of going green. It means using less energy, throwing less garbage away, and not wasting things.

A clothes dryer uses a lot of energy. Hanging clothes on a rack or clothesline is a good way to reduce energy.

Writing on both sides of a piece of paper reduces the amount of paper you use.

Take Action!

There are easy ways you and your family can reduce. Buy a large glass container of juice instead of little juice boxes. Conserve energy by putting on a sweater to keep warm instead of turning up the heat. Try to think of four other ways you and your family can reduce.

Reusing

Going green also means reusing items. Reusing means using something again, maybe in a different way. Reusing things makes the most of the time, money, materials, and energy used to make the items. It also creates less garbage that ends up buried in **landfills**.

Using old newspapers to wrap presents or putting pencils and markers in old cans are great ways to reuse items.

Give it away

Millions of people around the world do not have the money to buy clothes, shoes, and toys. Rather than throwing out items you no longer want, give them to someone who can use them!

Recycling

Recycling means changing or processing something so it can be used again. You can recycle a lot of things including cans, paper, glass, and plastic. All these things can be turned into many new products.

Old newspaper can be recycled to become egg cartons, kitty litter, construction paper, and many other things.

Take Action!

Does your family recycle? What do you recycle? Visit the website of your local recycling center to find out if there are more things that you can recycle!

Recycling waste

Food and yard waste can be recycled and turned into **compost**. Compost is waste, such as dead leaves or vegetable peels, that has broken down. Over time, compost changes into rich soil that helps plants grow.

Food and yard waste can be composted in backyard bins. When the compost changes to soil, it can be used in gardens.

Save trees

Trees are important to life on Earth. They take in **carbon dioxide** from the air and let out **oxygen** that living things need to breathe. They are homes for many animals and provide people with wood, paper, and foods including fruits, nuts, and seeds.

Timber companies cut down huge areas of forest. Often, trees are cut down faster than new trees can grow!

Take Action!

You can help save trees by reducing, reusing, and recycling all the paper products in your home. Make a list of other ways you and your family can go green by using the Three Rs.

Have separate boxes in your home for recycling different products. This can help you and your family remember what can be recycled.

Go green!

Anyone can go green. All you need is a little know-how. Review the different ways to go green in this book or research other ways on the Internet. Then, form a green group at your school or in your community.

Your green group can pick up garbage in the schoolyard or plant trees in the neighborhood.

Learning more

Books

Hirsch, Rebecca E. *Protecting Our Natural Resources*. Cherry Lake Publishing, 2010.

Kalman, Bobbie. *The ABCs of the Environment* (The ABCs of the Natural World). Crabtree Publishing Company, 2009.

Kondonassis, Yolanda. *Our House Is Round: A Kid's Book About Why Protecting Our Earth Matters*. Sky Pony Press, 2012.

Marshall, Laura K. *Being Green*. Wooden Tulip Press, 2013.

Websites

Greenpeace International

www.greenpeace.org/international

Earth 911: How Kids are Saving the Planet

http://earth911.com/news/2010/04/19/how-kids-are-saving-the-planet/

Earth Hour

www.earthhour.org/

Kids Be Green

http://kidsbegreen.org/

Words to know

Note: Some boldfaced words are defined where they appear in the book.

carbon dioxide (KAHR-buhn dahy-OK-sahyd) noun A gas made up of carbon and oxygen that is present in air

fossil fuels (FOS-uhl FYOO-uhlz) noun Fuels such as oil, natural gas, and coal that are used to power cars, make electricity, and heat and cool homes

fumes (fyoomz) noun Unpleasant smoke or gas

global warming (GLOH-buhl WAWRM-ing) noun The gradual increase in Earth's temperature

impact (IM-pakt) noun A strong or forceful effect

landfills (LAND-filz) noun Huge holes in the ground that are filled with garbage and then covered with soil

natural resources (NACH-er-uh-l REE-sawrs-ez) noun Useful materials, such as trees and water, that are found in nature

non-renewable (non-ri-NOO-a-buhl) adjective Referring to something that cannot be replaced

oxygen (OK-si-juhn) noun A gas present in air that humans, animals, and plants need to stay alive

pollution (puh-LOO-shuhn) noun Chemicals, fumes, waste, or garbage that harm or spoil Earth

recycle (ree-SAHY-kuhl) verb To change or process something to be used again, sometimes in a different way

reduce (ri-DOOS) verb To use or produce less

reuse (ree-YOOZ) verb To use something again

A *noun* is a person, place, or thing.
An *adjective* is a word that tells you what something is like.
A *verb* is an action word that tells you what someone or something does.

Index